THE VIEW FROM INSIDE

THE VIEW FROM INSIDE

Creating Your Own Calm

Donna Levesque

ISBN: 9781672880664

CONTENTS

INTRODUCTION

Adversity challenges what we think and believe. Pain makes us know what is true.

I have been told that the person who caused me the most pain in my life is my greatest teacher. I think each of us can effortlessly identify that person. I know I can. The thing about the lessons taught by our greatest teachers is that they have a profound effect, are not easily learned, and result in transformation or some kind of death. After watching me live through my pain, my son said to me, "I didn't know who you would become." Although my pain was death worthy, I believe that if I had not met and lived with this teacher of mine, I would not have learned what I am writing about in this book. I was transformed and now live a simpler, more peaceful, and content life. Simple but not small, peaceful but not without conflict, and content but with exciting adventures.

Words of advice and philosophies are easily spoken. We can read, watch videos, and listen to podcasts suggesting a bazillion methods to live our best life, with ways to solve our problems and find our purpose, happiness, and fulfillment. The truth is that we learn from living our lives, and all the choices we make are influenced by what we know in that moment in time. The information we read, see, and hear provides us with insight into new awareness, but ultimately it is our actions taken as a result of a decision that define our reality and character. We live to find our own unique answers to who we are and what matters to us. No two lives are the same. Circumstances may be similar, but our ever-evolving and unmatched perspectives guide how life is experienced. The answers to my life questions have little or no relevance to yours because who and what matters to each of us is different.

I am not writing anything that has not been written by someone else using their own words to express what they know. I write for the opportunity to make sense of what I have come to believe to be true for me through all that I have lived. I write to share what I know now that may help others with their personal pursuits for their own understanding. I write words much like an artist paints a picture, to inspire movement and life-enriching thoughts. I write to stimulate individual creativity, to encourage self-awareness, and, ultimately, to feel confidence. Because with confidence, anything is possible.

I live in New England, and when the winter season offers frigid temperatures, snow, wind, and rain, I am always grateful for the shelter of my home that protects me from the drama of the weather conditions. I can observe it and make my decisions as to how I will deal with it from a safe place.

I have found another home that provides similar benefits. I first accessed it when I sat with my pain, closed my eyes, and became conscious of my breath. I found a strange quiet that I now know exists in all of us. Once you find it, a most wonderful and unfamiliar sense of calm occurs. This connection is to our inner self that offers a safe haven from where to observe the world without experiencing the direct effects of it, much like looking out a window during a storm. The connection is with the consciousness of our wisdom that brings clarity about life, our best answers to the dilemmas we encounter, and the confidence and courage to live a full life no matter what happens. I now know that nothing outside me is more important than this loving, comforting, in-this-together, never-going-to-leave connection with myself.

UNION WITH SELF

There is an unimaginable comfort in becoming your own best friend, to cherish and value yourself in ways that you do others. Spiritual teachers often suggest that we must learn to love ourselves first to enable our ability to give and attract a healthy form of love.

I never understood what that meant or even how to love myself. How could I, knowing what I know about myself? I found it far too easy to criticize and reject myself for my intimate knowledge of past poor choices and regretful behavior that formed my own version of shame. Author Brené Brown defines shame as the intensely painful feeling or experience of believing that we are flawed and therefore unworthy of love and belonging—something we've experienced, done, or failed to do makes us unworthy of connection.

Our unresolved shame seems to fuel our creation of an inauthentic person we believe worthy of connection and love. We bury our flawed true self and all its beauty in the rubble of self-judgments, leaving us exhaustively living as a person we are not. Shame cannot survive in a person who loves and offers themselves empathy and forgiveness. To begin a union with self, we must discover an inner consciousness that silently observes our life as we live it without judgment of who we are or what we do. This observer is our personal source for comfort and encouragement to become our best selves. It is also the source for loving ourselves.

Our view of the world is transformed when we form an inner connection with and love for ourselves. We no longer think of ourselves as who we once were but who we are in this current moment, knowing the experiences of our past are but lessons to make our present moment better. Acceptance of every aspect of who we are in every moment positively affects our choices and attitude toward the circumstances of our lives. Becoming comfortable with feeling uncomfortable allows us to accept our lives with less resistance to what we don't want that can't be avoided. With love for ourselves and acceptance of our lives, we become more able to manage life's uncertainty and the constant and unpredictable changes that exist with living.

Like most people, I spent many years of my life looking for love, validation, inclusion, and acceptance from anyone outside myself. The intrinsic problem with this approach is that we betray who we are to align with someone else's views and opinions in hopes of being loved and included. We pretend to be someone we are not, with expectations of achieving the acceptance in the world we desire. We deem validation by others as our path to worthiness.

The only true influence we have in our lives is expressed by our choices. To make choices based on some else's worldview and not our own is an inauthentic life. This is commonly referred to as giving your power away. I think this way of being is the result of living our imperfect lives and believing that acceptance by others somehow mitigates the effects of our cumulative feelings of shame and regret. When we feel that we are important to someone else, we think for that moment we are good enough. When we become most important to ourselves, we are always good enough.

The poet Rumi advises, "We carry inside us the wonders that we seek outside us. The desire to know your soul will end all other desires." With self-awareness and love for ourselves, we gradually lose our need for outside validation of our worthiness. Until we learn that nothing matters more than living a life without concern for what another thinks of us, we continue to betray ourselves and we suffer.

Our human nature seeks inclusion in other people's lives, so I am not implying that we should live an isolated life and exclude all other perspectives and worldly success. We need to share our mutual interests with others, express contrasting points of view, and experience uncomfortable interactions to live fully and learn more about life and ourselves. It is through our met and unmet goals, interactions with other people, and contrasting personalities and perspectives that we create the opportunities to grow and learn. Sharing experiences and knowledge with others is life. It is with whom we choose to share our life experiences that define the quality of our lives and become a critical influence on our opportunities and well-being. The better we know, accept, and cherish ourselves, the easier it is to recognize and gravitate toward like-minded people.

It is also our common nature to want societal acceptance, but it is whose acceptance we seek that is significant. This brings us back to knowing and loving ourselves, which attracts who will love and accept us as we are. With these people, we feel comfortable to be who we are without filters. They are who matter because they allow us to be our authentic selves, which makes our relationships easy, safe, real, and honest. When we seek a relationship with our like-minded people, acceptance and validation exist organically. For me, if I can collapse from the weight of my life, be inappropriate, discuss my deepest thoughts and fears, and cry with you while feeling understood and without fear of gossip or judgment, then you are "my person." You are who matters outside me. Your opinions and thoughts have meaning in my life.

As our inner consciousness and a loving connection grow for ourselves, so do our confidence and courage in all our interactions. The better we know ourselves, the less we can be affected by other people's opinions of us. We know that we don't know, but our ability to differentiate what we believe is true and what is true becomes clear, as does an understanding of what is best for us. Our relationships with others are real and become less contentious. We grow to be our best selves by becoming most important to ourselves. By respecting and loving ourselves just as we are, we are able to love and respect others fully just as they are and without a transactional relationship built on expectations. We learn to trust our own inner wisdom with only a discerning interest in outside influences. We can be wrong without feeling shame, needing to assign blame, or avoiding responsibility for our mistakes.

No matter the depth of intimacy we have with another, the most incredible attribute of our inner connection is that no one else can access it. For each of us, it is our personal bond with our purest wisdom, and once we form this union with our truest eternal friend, we never feel alone in the world.

CHOOSE WISELY

In *The Power of Now,* Eckhart Tolle writes, "People don't realize that now is all there ever is; there is no past or future except as memory or anticipation in your mind." Similar to this, people don't realize that their lives are a series of choices; some are made with no conscious thought while others require thought and a deliberate decision. When we wake in the morning, our routines are made up of unconscious decisions, but the life-determining ones like whether to marry, where to live, whether to have a child, where to seek employment, who to cultivate as friends, or even how to respond to a contentious encounter define and have long-term influences on our lives.

The beginning circumstances of our lives and the resulting influences are predetermined. Where and to whom we are born and whether we are born into wealth or poverty, are healthy or ill, strong or weak, cherished or abused set the starting point from where we grow and learn. Determinism is a belief that our behavior is governed by these predetermined forces over which we have no control or the ability to influence. Oprah was born into poverty in rural Mississippi to a teenage single mother and is a significant example to challenge that, despite any circumstances we are born into or influenced by, we do have the ability to influence our lives toward changed circumstances simply by the choices we make.

Our choices move us from our starting point in life, develop our always evolving morals and priorities, and reflect what we know at the moment in our life when we are making the choice. Our personal integrity is the direct result of all our choices. We have no ability to affect where we start our lives, but we can influence our future.

Change occurs as a result of making different choices. We make different choices as we learn more about ourselves, society, and others. We know more just by living each day, which offers improved clarity and understanding about our preferences, personal goals, and perspectives of right and wrong. The hard part of choice is the internal conflict about the circumstance requiring a choice to be made. The right action is usually or maybe always more difficult while the less desirable choice will likely bring immediate relief from the internal conflict. The pain of addiction comes to mind. To choose not to indulge in addictive behavior is much more challenging than the immediate relief of succumbing to the addiction. Sometimes the better choice is not always obvious, or it can be a choice between the lesser of two wrongs, but the outcome will always be best with the intention of doing what is right.

British writer J. K. Rowling suggests, "It is our choices that show what we truly are, far more than our abilities." I, too, believe that everything about who we are is reflected in the choices we make. And likely the greatest contributors to the choices we make are our ability to accept and surrender to the circumstances of our lives while continuing to do our best and valuing ourselves. If we love and respect ourselves, we will not allow others not to. If we accept life as it is without resistance, we are less likely to continue to make choices that do not align with what is working in our lives.

The common theme of sacred books like the Bible, the Torah, the Bhagavad Gita, and the Koran is our free will to choose. These ancient texts use dramatic worldly circumstances to demonstrate life challenges. But ultimately the allegories described in all these books promote resolution of our internal conflicts while encouraging us to choose right over wrong and good over evil.

Our choices at all times reflect who we are, what we know and believe, and how we feel and ultimately define how we will live in the world. Our choices are not as simple as right or wrong. They are the strength of our courage, compassion, and empathy; who and what is important to us; our priorities in life; our discipline; our ability to forgive; and our attitude toward our personal circumstances. These attributes are constantly changing. The more we live, the more we learn about ourselves, the world, and others. We can choose not to make life harder than it has to be just by being conscious of the consequences of the choices we make.

There are no wrong choices because all our choices lead to experiences that provide us with the opportunity to know more. Beloved writer Maya Angelou advises, "Do the best you can until you know better. Then when you know better, do better." Doing is the action of our choices, so to live well, we must choose wisely.

NOTHING MORE

Love is another one of those words that means something different to everyone. We seem to know more about what love is not than what it is. We are confident about what we do not love, but we question how to and if we actually do love. It is not logical, and like all feelings, it ebbs and flows. It is a feeling fueled by emotion from a myriad of sources. A love interest, an innocent animal, your newborn baby, or a stranger in need all stimulate a different kind and depth of love. When we try to understand, ignore, question, or judge love for its merits, we diminish or lose the feeling. The truth is that love makes us vulnerable. And it seems that we will do pretty much anything to avoid feeling vulnerable.

What is love? Love for another person allows us to feel pleasure for their joy and success. Love always offers understanding, forgiveness, and encouragement. Love is the willingness to listen and compromise. How do we sustain love for another amid the constant changes we experience as we learn more about ourselves and life? It seems that love requires a commitment to love despite the never-ending obstacles life creates to threaten it. Love may be magical at first light, but thereafter it is a choice and a conscious recommitment to love or to let it go.

I am certain that when the Dalai Lama proclaimed that love was his religion, he was not speaking about romantic love but compassion and respect for all humanity. I imagine that the love he speaks of is an unconditional love for anyone he encounters without any type of discrimination.

The unavoidable aspect of love is the certainty for future heartache and loss through death, divorce, separation, or illness. Love always has an ending, but even with this certain inevitability, we seek to love and be loved. This is how important love is to our existence. There is nothing that can more profoundly affect anyone's life than love.

Taking a risk to love someone requires mutual honesty and vulnerable interactions, which create the opportunity for trust and respect to grow. For love to flourish, trust and respect must exist. Self-love is no different. It requires honest and constant introspection with respect, compassion, acceptance, forgiveness, and trust in the truthfulness of decisions and actions.

I believe that love is the foundation for serenity, has the capacity to resolve and heal problems, and allows acceptance of all diversity. It comforts, soothes, inspires, excites, energizes, feeds motivation and seems to envelop all that is perfect in our world. Nothing we do that originates from love can be harmful or hurtful to ourselves or anyone else. Love is devoid of prejudice, fear, and hate. The love I am describing is not a fleeting feeling but a commitment and discipline to be a loving person. From love comes the ability to feel joy, to be lighthearted, to laugh, and to relax in the security it creates. With love, we can find courage to do what is best amid our conflicts and challenges.

The Five Love Languages by Gary Chapman suggests that love is expressed and experienced in several ways, with each of us having a specific preference. Love is shown by giving gifts, being attentive, speaking words of affirmation and affection, being devoted, and touching. When we love ourselves in the way we prefer, our personal need for love is fulfilled, making any loving gesture from another perfect.

Albert Einstein states, "Everything is energy and that's all there is to it. Match the frequency of the reality you want, and you cannot help but get that reality. It can be no other way. This is not philosophy. This is physics." Perhaps when we choose to be loving, we attract love and spread love.

In the song "Imagine," my favorite Beatle, John Lennon, asks us to imagine a life of peace, with all people living as one. To imagine this, there has to be universal love, and just maybe, love is all we need and nothing more.

MYOB

A familiar parable of Jesus often quoted as good advice is to "live and let live." The twenty-first-century expression for this sentiment is more likely to be "mind your own business," which is commonly referred to in my family as MYOB. My interpretation of to live and let live is to live without judging others or taking hurtful action against another. Equally difficult, MYOB means not offering an opinion about another person's life or engaging in any form of gossip. The obstacle is our society's growing preference for voyeuristic reality TV and the popularity of social media. Both distract us from minding our own business; knowing more about someone else's life has no relevance to what is happening in our own lives. It is a questionable use of our precious time, and when doing so, it is likely wise to use Edgar Allen Poe's good advice as a filter: "Believe nothing you hear (in this case read) and only half of what you see." And more importantly, we should follow these guidelines from Buddha: "Believe nothing, no matter where you read it, or who said it, no matter if I have said it unless it agrees with your own reason and your own common sense."

In its simplest form, MYOB means not talking about another person or anything about their life. Gossip is the opposite of MYOB. It is how we waste time and avoid progress in our own lives.

It is much easier to look at someone else's life and form seemingly automatic opinions and judgments as to their best action to take rather than to face our own unresolved challenges. I have often wondered why I think I can look at another person's life and feel confident in knowing what is best for that person. I can't possibly know what is best for another person, not even my children. How each of us experiences the world is different. Our priorities, views of the world, skills, and desires are unique and influence all our actions. Most importantly, when we look at someone else's challenges, we are seeing them without feeling the emotions that have affected their decisions and actions. Our emotions affect everything. At a point in my life, it was obvious that I needed to divorce, but I couldn't because my emotions about my marriage paralyzed me, despite knowing that divorce was the better choice for me.

Tuning into another person's life is the most common form of self-distraction and fuels the ill-advised practice of comparing to feel better or worse than another. My friend told me that she stayed married because after listening to me talk about my marriage, her marriage didn't seem so bad. We are both divorced. Comparisons are dangerous and serve no good purpose.

What is happening to someone really has nothing to do with anyone else other than how the circumstances may affect them. Parents divorcing affects their children, a person dying affects those who love them, and a child arrested affects the parents, but ultimately these things happen only to the person living the experience. I am not suggesting that we don't care about others, and we can offer the voice of our own wisdom when asked, but each of us, even our children, walk our own unique path that is created by our choices.

The truth is that we can never know what someone else is thinking or feeling about anything. We also can never know what has been said to influence what another may think of us or how our words and behavior are interpreted, nor should it matter. This is why what we think about ourselves is far more important than what anyone else is thinking about us. Our peace of mind, contentment, and confidence can be directly correlated to our ability not to be influenced by other people's thoughts or opinions about who we are or the circumstances of our lives. We are all on a lone journey with a few fellow travelers who become our trusted friends along the way.

MYOB is freedom and an integral part of living a conscious life, being with yourself, and making yourself and your unique circumstances most important to you. This mindfulness promotes healthy individuality and encourages our own responsibility for the quality of our lives and respect for others. It is suggested that each of us is responsible for our own happiness and fulfillment in life. This is achieved by increasing our self-awareness, which enables an authentic and healthy relationship with others. The better we know, accept, and love ourselves, the better our relationships become.

We are all living unique lives on lone paths but share common goals to feel that we are good enough and to live in peace, confidence, and contentment, free from angst, doubt, and confusion. Each of us learns from our life experiences, which leaves us with our own understanding about how to best live. There are many books about the meaning and purpose of life, how to find happiness and fulfillment, and some suggestions about how to live. We cannot find our answers in any book because our answers about life and how to live are for each of us to experience and determine for ourselves. We find our precious answers for living our life with a consciousness and willingness to learn from our experiences.

The three gates of speech—Is it true, is it necessary, and is it kind?—may be the best advice for minding our own business. If we use this criteria, we will likely speak less and listen more. We speak what we know and listen to know more.

A SELF-REVOLUTION

The degree of violence in any society is related to the degree of inequality between its wealthy and poor. We cannot settle for societal measurement of superiority, strength, or success based on monetary wealth and power. This measurement for success ignores the large majority of the self-reliant but unwealthy that form and sustain the foundation from which anyone's monetary wealth is possible. Our world seems to think that wealth and celebrity are significant attributes of success and value. It is this material mindset that feeds scarcity and greed and that now influences the consciousness of our world and gives the microphone and spotlight to those with the most money. We have learned that a presidency can be bought and that wrongdoings can be overlooked—second chances given for anyone with enough money. This is not a new problem. A 1960's comic strip, *The Wizard of Id*, offered the satirical insight that the golden rule is that he who has the gold makes the rules.

Unfortunately for those of us without monetary wealth and a voice to influence, our attention has been manipulated to a focus of constant crises and public debates with the sole purpose of assigning blame. The unsettling awareness of wrongdoings and war has become commonplace. The unending focus on what is wrong feeds a malignant fear of the potentiality of what will be. The unresolved conflicts, the awareness of unpunished wrongdoings, and the fear of uncertainty are crippling. Through a myriad of media outlets comes a relentless onslaught of the injustices in our world. These sensationalized distractions hold our attention, and we have lost sight of what is good about humanity. World news leaves us feeling overwhelmed by the enormity of the problems without actionable solutions. This confusion of not knowing what to do is predominant in our society and cultivates apathy based on strong feelings of individual powerlessness to influence change.

It seems obvious that we cannot settle for living in a world with a morality riddled with unconsciousness and the avoidance of individual accountability. We have lost sight of what makes life meaningful and what sustains us best through conflicts that are inherent with being alive—that is, doing the next right thing. I realize that the next right thing is not always obvious, and it can also be a choice between the lesser of two wrong things, but the intention of doing what is right will always result in the best outcome.

You or I alone can't change the world, but we can become a better version of ourselves as we live each day. And if each of us does this, the world will be changed by our collective consciousness. The paradox is that collectively the silenced unwealthy and seemingly powerless majority truly have the power to create change.

How do we become better versions of ourselves? I am certain that having asked yourself this question, an intention has been set into motion and you will find your own answers simply because you have asked. I offer my personal answers to this question to stimulate your own thoughts.

- Love yourself and become your own best friend because once you have a connection with yourself, you don't have the need to pretend to be someone you are not, nor is there a need to seek fulfillment from outside yourself.

- Think for yourself, make your own choices, form your own conclusions, and know when you are being manipulated.

- Choose forgiveness when you can; when you can't, choose acceptance so that you can move past unencumbered by what you deem unforgivable.

- Love others with compassion, knowing that life is not easy for anyone.

- Listen more than you speak.

- Master self-discipline with flexibility.

- Be defenseless amid criticism. Determine what is useful and forget the rest.

- Know that acceptance of every moment just as it is can minimize suffering.

- Make your choices in life with the conscious intent of choosing right over wrong, no matter how hard it is to do the right thing.

- Know when your insecurities are limiting your life and do what you fear.

- Let your past positively inform who you are today because your past no longer exists and who you were then doesn't either.

- No matter the circumstances, assume responsibility for all you say and do and know that assigning blame achieves nothing.

- Realize that shame limits life and great things can be achieved when we are willing to be vulnerable.

- Grasp the concept that there is no one else like you in the world. Your uniqueness is what makes you special.

- Whatever they are, share your gifts freely with others.

- Know that we are all the same, we are here to learn, no one has an easy ride, and every person has value in the world.

- Become extraordinary by loving your life, despite its many annoyances.

- No one of us is better than another, no matter what we look like, how we speak, or what we do.

- Be honest with yourself and all others because honesty allows you freedom to be who you are.

IS THIS ALL THERE IS?

Despite knowing that living in this moment with gratitude for all that exists ensures that I will live my best life, I still find myself asking, "Is this all there is?" It seems that I want more than what exists for me, and I can't even identify what is the more that I desire.

Like every child born, I have survived the perils of my childhood and continue to learn from my experiences. I have birthed and raised four children to adulthood, with all the responsibilities, challenges, worries, joys, and desires associated with parenting. I found my way into and out of two marriages. These rich life experiences have taught me about gratitude, betrayal, love, beauty, fear, ignorance, indecision, humility, patience, anticipation, disappointment, compromise, confidence, hate, jealousy, abandonment, humiliation, acceptance, addiction, and mental illness. But when I think about my life, still I ask, is this all there is?

After traveling to India, I know without a doubt that my life is full and blessed with more than enough of everything. I live a very desirable life amid remarkable diverse friendships, kind and loving children, and loyal animals. I am physically fit and healthy. My mind is clear, and I have lived long enough to be a wise woman, but still I ask for more. What makes me want more?

Is it the routine of life that leaves me asking for more? Is it the certainty of each day, with obligations and time-consuming chores that influence me to want more of something that will make my life extraordinary? Is it that I don't feel special or successful enough or that I don't have enough? My favorite of the Tao Te Ching's wisdom is this: "When you realize what you have is enough, you are truly rich." I do have enough, so this wanting for more must be my personal expression of greed.

Greed is described as an excessive desire for and attachment to money, power, or possessions. The desire for better and more are best friends in the world of wanting. The insatiable desire that accompanies greed creates anxiety and restlessness. There seems to be a belief that if we obtain more of what we already have or if we acquire what we want, life will be better and we will be happy. Our unfortunate belief that the elusive state of happiness can be achieved from something the material world has to offer.

This thinking reminds me of my favorite children's book by Shel Silverstein, *The Giving Tree.* In pursuit of his endless desire for worldly happiness, the boy greedily takes from the tree and then abandons it until he wants something more from the tree. Loving the boy and wanting him to be happy, the tree willingly gives the boy his apples for money, his branches for a house, and finally his trunk for a boat, leaving the tree reduced to a mere stump. At the end of the boy's life, he returns to the tree an exhausted and unfulfilled man, finding contentment in the simplicity of a quiet place to sit and rests on the stump of the tree. Mr. Silverstein seems to be suggesting that until we are exhausted by our endless pursuit for material possessions and the distraction of wanting more, we are blind to the gifts of rest and the life that exist without this yearning.

Greed does not allow contentment, and as love heals all the ills of our world, greed gives life to all the evils of our humanity. Excessive greed builds a willingness to compromise our morals and values and distorts our perception of acceptable behaviors.

It reduces our appreciation for what matters most, which is the importance and quality of our relationships. I can think of no atrocity in our world that when stripped to its core beginnings is not founded in some sort of greed. Greed is the predator of world peace and personal contentment.

Gratitude is the antivenom for greed. The symptoms of greed weaken our gratitude for the most important blessings in our lives. There is much about life to be grateful for that has nothing to do with acquisition and is far more valuable than what we have, where we live, or who we know. Gratitude for our ability to talk, see, hear, walk, taste, breathe, and interact easily with others is overlooked and exists unacknowledged until lost. If we can live each day with gratitude for what does exist, then is this all there is will always be enough.

LOSE THE BATTLE

Every major life journey or challenge in our world today tends to be portrayed as a competition against something or someone to be won. Rather than calmly working toward a solution, seeing it as an opportunity to grow and learn or finding out how to best deal with something or someone, we react, resist, justify, blame, and fight. We fight to prove we are right, wrestle with our weight, battle anxiety and depression, succumb to illness, avenge a perceived wrongdoing, resist diversity, and debate equality for all. The truth is that for each and every one of us, life is filled with disagreements, conflicts, and, sometimes, crippling challenges that always cause some level of confusion and pain. Maybe it's the seemingly unfair or unexpected challenges we have experienced that have caused us to often feel hostile, ready for a fight. Maybe the challenges have caused so much pain that we are constantly in a defensive mode and everyday annoyances have become intolerant. Maybe it's just the comparative inequities of life and our pride needing to win, to be right, or to feel good enough.

The need for self-importance makes comparison and competition commonplace in our world and is used as a frame of reference to attempt to find our place in an egocentric world. When a person's view of themselves is built on comparisons and competitiveness, life becomes like a battleground. This path guarantees suffering due to its dependency on the always wavering ego's involvement in determining the following questions: Am I better? Did I win? Am I viewed by the world as successful? A life built on this form of pride is a life driven by an unleashed, fear-based, doubt-filled, emotionally driven ego and can never be the foundation for a stable and satisfying life. A prideful life is the direct opposite of a life lived with humility and grace.

Humility is defined as a low view of one's importance when actually it is the opposite. Humility is soulful confidence in one's value accompanied by respect for all others. Real wisdom develops from the honesty offered by this unassuming personality trait. To live a humble life illustrates a confident self-esteem, personal integrity, and reverence for humanity. A humble person is not seeking and does not need validation from anyone or anything outside themselves. It is the foundation for living an authentic life based on self-awareness and acceptance. Humility allows the willingness to learn from every interaction without the limitations of a judgment of or resistance to an experience or person. It is a freedom from any need to pretend to be someone we are not. The ability to be humble is a reflection of a strong and healthy inner connection.

A life lived with humility gives birth to grace. Grace is the unconditional acceptance of life and others just as it is and as they are. It allows personal failure without shame, achievement without the need for acknowledgment, and compassion for all humanity. The Christian-based phrases "rest in God's grace" and "by the grace of God" are used to describe a source for comfort and blessing granted by God to an individual in a time of need. It can be an illness healed, finding something lost, words spoken to ease painful emotions, or anything that mitigates a simple or excruciating challenge. Our human expressions of grace are demonstrated when we offer loving compassion to another without regard to the circumstances that created the need or the character of the person in need. It can be as simple as a smile to a stranger, an anonymous donation to a charity, or gracing someone with forgiveness for a minor or profound wrongdoing.

Humility is the silence of wisdom with no need to be right or to assume a dominant position in any circumstance. Acts of grace are a choice and are offered to another without reciprocity or fear of what others will think. There are endless battles and painful injuries in a pride-driven life. There can be no battles when humility and grace exist.

ACTIONS WITHOUT EXPECTATIONS

The spectrum of human emotions, from feelings of a desperate need to gluttonous greed, seems to make it difficult to live without expectations. Expectations envelope all our needs, wants, and desires, whether they be from a person, an experience, an event, or an acquisition. Suffering occurs when we believe that we are deserving of something and we don't get it. Our options are to wallow in our perceived misfortune while continuing attempts to have our expectations realized or accepting that what we wanted or thought would occur did not. The truth is that there is nothing we can do that makes us deserving or not deserving; we simply get what we get. The only cure for the suffering associated with unmet expectations is acceptance. Acceptance of what it is we do not want is not an ending but more a beginning of allowing life to present itself in ways we never imagined.

We live mostly in a transactional world comprised of what we will receive in return for our actions. If I pay you money, you will provide a service or product that meets my expectations. If I eat healthy foods and exercise, I will be fit and live a long life. If I love you, then you will love me, or because I love you, you cannot die. A much harder expectation to reconcile is when we don't have what we want but we believe that we deserve it. Deserving is a belief that we are entitled to a reward, praise, or acknowledgment. The feeling that we are deserving profoundly influences our life expectations. Every human being is worthy. Each of us contributes something just by being alive, giving us implicit worth and value in the world. We are all worthy, but in reality, we deserve nothing.

Unmet expectations create the greatest vulnerability to feelings of resentment, jealousy, and—worse—resistance to our individual reality. These ill feelings are painful. It becomes an internal war between resistance to and acceptance of what is versus how we want our lives to be or what we want. And there can be no denying that a war of any kind promises pain.

This brings us back to the certainty that we have no control over the outcome of our actions. Our actions are the result of our choices, and from there we simply free fall through the resulting consequences. The only effect we can have is to consciously exercise our free will to choose and take actions with blind acceptance of the outcome. Our free will-fueled choices and actions will influence the paths of our lives. We get to choose what we will do, whether it be climbing a mountain, speed racing, practicing yoga, running a marathon, reading, or watching television. To live peacefully, it becomes imperative that we choose wisely in all we do and that we speak with accountability and acceptance of the outcome. We must accept the outcome of our actions without judgments that it is good or bad, a success or a failure, or not what we want. Buddhists refer to this as nirvana, the state in which there is neither suffering nor desire.

Worry is a crippling feeling and, like anticipation, is another aspect of expectations. Anticipation can be a positive expectation while worry is an imagined future that may be what we do not want to exist. These two feelings are the foundation for anxiety; they are thoughts about a future we cannot influence because it does not exist and may never exist. Worry removes the possibility of peace.

A Buddha teaching that aligns with these thoughts is that "peace begins when expectations end." As with all logical conclusions and new awareness, the challenge is doing it. Knowing is never enough; we must do.

Making decisions and taking actions while allowing life to unfold without resistance to the outcome is the beginning of losing expectations of ourselves, others, and life. Taking action without expectations allows the possibility that what we think we want can become exactly what we don't want and that what we get that we didn't want can become exactly what it is we need.

DANGER OF JUDGMENTS AND THE GIFT OF FORGIVENESS

To live completely without judgment is impossible. Despite their high potential for flaws, our judgments are the key ingredient to our opinions, which significantly influence our choices. To choose wisely, we need to be wise and discerning judges.

Each judgment we make is formed by what we believe to be true about life, ourselves, and others. Judgments seem to form in our thoughts automatically, without a prior conscious decision to judge. Have you ever looked at a stranger and formed an immediate opinion as to their character just by their physical appearance? Have you ever watched someone interact in a situation and turned away shaking your head? Have you ever said, "I would never do that"? These impulsive judgments based on limited information are at the heart of all prejudice. We are judging how something or someone appears based on assumptions or on what we believe to be true without any proof. Assumptions are a product of our feelings and are factless thoughts that can falsely influence our understanding of what is actually true. Becoming conscious of our human nature to judge and the significance of it in our lives makes it important that we learn to be open-minded and question our judgments. Recognizing that we judge almost every aspect of our lives to no advantage is the beginning of being more conscious about how and when we judge. It is unlikely that we will ever stop judging, but the more we live without preferences, the less we will react to our random judgments.

Judgments that do not allow acceptance are a major obstacle to forgiving. Murder, rape, abuse of any kind against another, acts of war, or any act with evil intent are examples of abominations against humanity that are most unforgivable. The victims of these atrocities have no responsibility in what occurred, but, unfortunately, finding a way to heal and move on does become the victim's responsibility. Forgiveness does not eliminate the painful memories, but the willingness to consider, if not forgiveness, then acceptance of what occurred, sets in motion an empowering healing process. This willingness allows the possibility that one day the memories will be less crippling and the associated pain can diminish. Forgiveness does not make what occurred less wrong but offers the promise that the victim's life won't forever be defined by another's action against them.

Forgiveness is a conscious, deliberate action to choose to remove the importance of something that was done or not done that requires forgiveness. It is not forgetting, excusing, or condoning an offense. The awareness gained from life experiences that requires forgiveness allows us to be able to accept or forgive and frees us from continued suffering over something we cannot change.

Forgiveness is about the past. When we are unable to forgive, we are tethered to that moment, unable to move forward unencumbered by emotional thinking of that experience. It becomes the contents of the metaphoric suitcase that we carry with us wherever we go, filling it with all our regretful, humiliating, painful, and unresolved experiences that we have accumulated while living our lives. Because life is filled with unending challenges, the suitcase can become very heavy if we can't let go easily. We learn how to live better by resolving the contrast and adversity encountered in the moment as we live each day of our lives for all our lives. Every experience we live has lessons for us to grow our awareness about ourselves and life. Circumstances requiring forgiveness can be of a magnitude that is unforgivable. This is when we strive for acceptance and consciously refuse to allow a past event or person to affect the present moments of our lives. With the acceptance of every aspect of our lives, we are free and can leave that suitcase filled with the pain of our lives behind. If not, we will be forever attached to the obsessive thoughts and resentments that imprison us to someone or something in our past that can't be undone.

Upon his release from prison after serving twenty-seven years for simply protesting against the South African government's racial segregation and discrimination policies, Nelson Mandela said, "As I walked out the door toward the gate that would lead to my freedom, I knew if I didn't leave my bitterness and hatred behind, I'd still be in prison." The less we react to our judgments, the better we are able to allow life to just be without resistance. The more conscious we become, the more easily we can accept what is and what has been, without letting it define our lives or who we are. This is freedom.

THE PRESENT MOMENT: ALL THAT IS GONE AND WHAT WILL BE

Living in the moment is the most popular advice about how to best live. Living in the moment is a mind empty of thoughts about anything other than what we are doing in that single moment. I fall short of this good advice because I often find myself distracted by ruminating thoughts of past experiences, what I need or want to do, or something that I don't understand. Unfortunately for me, I can add this failure to my long list of self-criticism that is readily available to me when I want to hold on to a bad mood.

An extreme example of living in the moment describes the process of washing your hands as a single focus. You observe your hand moving toward the faucet, then touching the faucet and turning it on, looking at the flowing water, moving your hands to the water, and so on, until the action is complete. I can't seem to stay focused long enough to write the whole process. Nor do I want to. I like my busy mind, and I also enjoy when my mind is quiet. More important to me than finding the discipline to focus on the present moment is the ability to choose my focus based on my priorities. When I am washing the dishes, I am uninterested in being in the moment and enjoy my random thoughts, but when I am talking with my grandson, my mind is focused on the flow of our conversation and its content. Being in the moment requires an interest in being in that moment, and not all moments of my life interest me enough to make them my single focus.

Eckhart Tolle suggests that life is a series of present moments, that there is nothing else ever but an endless series of now. This is unquestionably logical, but how does one constantly live in the now without moments of reflection and feeling anticipation? My thoughts of other moments serve to influence what I am doing and will be doing. Learning to live in the moment while observing random thoughts and consciously not allowing any attention to the thoughts that do not serve a productive purpose seems to be a better goal than striving to live in a moment completely devoid of past or future thoughts.

Overthinking and assigning emotional labels to a thought about the past causes depression while expectations of or overfixating on the future create feelings of anxiety. At my best, I am conscious of my random thinking and attempt to observe the thought without attaching emotion or judgment to it. When I am able to do this, the thought passes and is replaced with another. Allowing thoughts to come and go while maintaining a positive attitude toward thoughts from the past for what was learned and accepting that we can never know what will be is a way to live in the present with less stress.

There is a time when we can easily live in the moment. It is when we are doing something we truly enjoy or learning something that is of great interest to us. In these moments, our minds are focused and empty of distracting thoughts. We become completely focused on what we are doing, with all our attention flowing toward the activity. Time passes unnoticed, and hours seem like minutes. It can be anything at all but it is what captures us. To know what we are passionate about is a gift, and when we know what that is, we can easily live in the present moment by choice and not because we should.

Our future depends on what we do today, so there can be no disputing that our pasts influence our lives in the present moment. Our unique one-of-a-kind perspective is formed by all that has been. There is no ability to relive or affect anything that has been because it no longer exists. It is futile to attempt to recreate a past experience that was then enjoyed or to fix a circumstance that now cannot be undone. Apologizing for or rectifying a past misdeed does not undo what has been done. It demonstrates only that we have learned from a mistake. All that has gone on before is done. Reflecting on our past offers only the opportunity to recognize the lessons learned to best influence our choices and actions with the potential of making the present moment better.

CHANGE, SURRENDER, AND FAITH

Change gives birth each day to movement and is the facilitator of growth. Although often resisted, it is obvious that everything about life changes from subtle, such as when a new song plays on the radio, to sudden, such as an unavoidable accident or profound death. Nothing ever stays as it once was, nor is there any promise of what will be.

For those who seek certainty in their lives, the uncertainty that accompanies constant change can be crippling. A greater aspect of impermanence is realizing that we have no actual control over anything about our lives. At the most, we can influence the paths of our lives through our choices, but, ultimately, we never know with any certainty what will result from our choices.

When we accept the absence of certainty and realize our inability to control any aspects of our lives, our best choice is to surrender to life just as it is and whatever it will be. Surrender is often thought of as a weakness and or as cowardice, but rather it is the strength to be brave enough to walk through life knowing that you don't know and can't know. Just by living, you will learn more to make choices that will better influence the framework of your life.

Resistance is the enemy of surrender. Surrendering is to accept life as it is without resistance. It is simply the choice between allowing life to unfold or to resist life as it is unfolding. Author Eckhart Tolle writes, "To offer no resistance to life is to be in the state of grace, ease, and lightness. What could be more insane than to create inner resistance to what already is? Surrender to life as it is and see how life suddenly starts working for you rather than against you." Michael A. Singer, the author of *The Surrender Experiment*, suggests a paradox that "if you are resisting something, you are feeding it. If you are pushing something away, you are actually inviting it to stay."

Surrender can happen automatically when life is excruciatingly painful and it becomes the only option. It can also be the result of an unexpected event or a long-term pattern of living, but in either case, it is ending the resistance to what is not as we want it to be. When we are no longer able to think of or envision any way to gain our desired outcome and cannot live another moment as we have been, we surrender to life as it is happening. The desire to end the pain and suffering created by the way we are living becomes the greater priority.

Oddly, the circumstances causing the pain don't change at the moment of surrender, but what occurs is a relief from the painful feelings of resisting the flow of life. A sense of peace forms from surrendering to life as it is, with a respite from the pursuit of something that is unachievable. Our thoughts offer the false belief that we can control our life circumstances. Surrender becomes an awareness that our lives are influenced only by our choices and that the resulting outcome is not something we can predict with any certainty, nor can we control it.

Martin Luther King Jr. said, "Faith is taking the first step even when you don't see the whole staircase." Taking the first step requires faith that life is not random, that there are no coincidences, and that each of us is living unique circumstances for a purpose we cannot know. Surrender gives birth to a belief in something more and greater than ourselves. Faith is the beginning of a spiritual life from which surrender and acceptance can grow with uncertainty becoming more tolerable.

Faith without an association with religion simply represents a belief in something unseen and greater than humanity. A parable of Jesus, "The kingdom of God is within you," suggests that God is part of each of us. When we have faith in God, we are able to find faith in ourselves.

The simplest concept of God is our awareness that there is right and wrong, good and evil, compassion and mercilessness, love and hate. The awareness of these virtues guides our choices and ultimately influences the content of our lives. Saint Thomas Aquinas writes, "To one who has faith, no explanation is necessary. To one without faith, no explanation is possible."

Faith is not a concept that once learned is known. It is a belief that grows as our commitment to having faith grows. More simply, as our faith grows, our fears weaken. And the less fear we have, the more easily we are able to live with confidence that no matter what happens, we will be fine. Victor Hugo's metaphor for life seems appropriate: "Be like the bird that, passing on her flight awhile on boughs too slight, feels them give way beneath her, and yet sings, knowing that she hath wings." Faith gives us wings to be confident and courageous amid constant change and life's uncertainty.

ABOUT OUR BODY

Our bodies are an extraordinary masterpiece and are undoubtedly the most complex organisms on Earth. We can breathe, think, speak, see, hear, smell, taste, walk, run, and climb; our bones are stronger than concrete; our gray matter is the most evolved brain in the animal kingdom; and we have the miraculous capacity to grow a life. All this and still there is more. Our remarkable bodies have the ability to survive profound adversity and can emotionally and physically heal themselves. Recognizing the greatness of our body can only encourage us to properly and consciously feed it with foods to keep it nourished, exercise it to remain strong and fit, and commit to continually grow and learn intellectually and spiritually for all the days of our lives. Our bodies fueled by our breath give us life.

Like all matter, the human body consists exclusively of atoms. The physical body is unique because it is the only energy field of the body that can be seen and touched. Surprisingly, it consists of only 0.01 percent of our whole body, with the remaining 999.99 percent unseen and untouchable. The four additional layers of energy that surround the physical body are where our unique mental, spiritual, and emotional characteristics are stored. They are not seen as easily as the physical body and collectively are referred

45

to as a person's aura. Basically, these five layers of energy define a human body. The four unseen layers of energy are the ethereal, which holds our highest standards for existence; the emotional, where emotionally charged experiences are regulated; the mental, where ideas, thoughts, and beliefs are processed; and the spiritual, where our highest consciousness resides.

Along the spinal column, there are seven circular vortexes of energy called chakras, meaning wheels. It is important that the chakras are open and that they rotate. Closed or blocked chakras contribute to difficulty concentrating, and feelings of fear, helplessness, indecision and apathy. Each of the seven chakras is associated with different aspects of life. The first chakra (the base of the spine) is related to survival and fear; the second (below the navel) to sexuality, creativity, and guilt; the third (above the navel) to self-confidence and shame; the fourth (the heart) to love and grief; the fifth (the throat) to self-expression and lies; the sixth (the middle of the forehead) to imagination and illusion; and the seventh (the crown of the head) to the connection to universal energy and attachment. It is through conscious breathing, movement, and sound that we are able to regulate the chakras.

Only when you exhale properly and fully can you breathe out toxins, like carbon dioxide, and allow fresh oxygen to flow back in. We can change our lives for the better just by consciously breathing. Breathing will calm anxiety and energize us. Conscious breathing and the breathing that occurs with movement and exercise keep the energy fields of our body flowing, which enriches our emotional and physical well-being. Conversely, a sedentary lifestyle creates a heavy, stagnant energy field that adversely affects our health. Our bodies need to move.

OUR THREE BRAINS

The brain in our head is the part of our body that gives us the ability to see, talk, hear, smell, and think. It is our body's action center, our consciousness, our logical and intellectual thought, including the memories and knowledge learned from all our life experiences. Its job is to maintain stability by correcting imbalances within our whole body and to ensure our physical safety.

Together the brain and spinal cord make up the communication system of our body. It uses a simple but intricate nerve system to carry sensory information from the rest of the body to the brain. The brain uses this system to send instructions to the entire body for movement, to regulate organ functions, and to manage responses to emotional experiences.

Brain signals instruct our hearts to pump blood throughout our bodies. Our heart rhythm constantly sends messages to the brain about our emotional state. Erratic, fast, or slow heartbeats reflect our emotional experiences in the present moment. The benefit of meditation is that our heartbeat slows, sending messages to our brain that indicate emotional stability. Oddly, the heart can continue to pump without the brain, but the brain cannot function without the heart, suggesting that the heart has its own brain.

Have you ever made a decision based on your gut feelings, without tangible information or knowledge to support your decision? Have you ever described nervousness as butterflies in your stomach? These are signals that you are receiving from your gut brain. This brain matter controls digestion and is found in the walls of our digestive system. The thoughts we experience from our gut brain are commonly referred to as our intuition. Intuition is believing that something is true without evidence.

The brain in our head offers logical thought about what we know, the brain in our heart influences how we feel, and our gut brain influences our decisions regarding what we believe to be true. Using any one of our brains alone can result in a less desirable decision, such as someone who knows logically (head) through behavior patterns that their relationship is abusive and believes (gut) the abuse will continue unless something changes but stays in the relationship because their decision is being exclusively governed by feelings (heart). Our life-altering decisions are best made when we consciously use the benefits of our three brains, the wisdom of our sacred voice with motivation offered by a submissive ego.

OUR TWO VOICES

I t is not our life but our thoughts about our life that cause our
emotions. The quality of our thoughts influences everything
about our lives. Each of us experiences life separately through
our thoughts. I am often surprised at the contrasting perspectives
when I listen to my children speak about a single shared event and
how it affected them. Our unique perspective about anything is
the direct result of the evolution of our thoughts, which are influenced by what each of us currently knows, feels, and believes.

I can identify two separate voices that define my thoughts. One
seems to chatter incessantly as I am living my life. It speaks about
my problems, the unfairness of what is happening in my life, what
I need to do to get what I want, and unappreciative thoughts; it
judges and attempts to motivate me into action using fear. This
voice also has the skill to make comparisons; it can determine that
I am better than and not good enough in a split second. This is the
harsh and critical voice of my insatiable ego that is constantly seeking acknowledgment and a sense of self-importance in the world.
The single goal of meditation is to quiet this voice to allow for a
less defensive and reactive existence. An uncontrolled ego has the
potential to make life very difficult. It is like a strobe light that
cycles back and forth, seeking confirmation of scarcity and danger

49

and evidence that our life is not, cannot, and will never be as we want it to be. The main goal of the ego is to motivate us to take an action—any action—but when our ego is motivated by scarcity and fear, our choices are often self-serving, immature, impulsive, and defensive.

The second voice of my thoughts is less boisterous and difficult to access when my ego is running wild. I can hear it easily when I slow down, pause, and breathe and especially when I close my eyes without sleep. When I am able to access it, I am soothed, feel confident in the wisdom it offers me, and believe it is the source for my well-being. I refer to it as my sacred voice. This sacred voice speaks to me about gratitude, encourages me toward acceptance and surrender, quiets my resistance, and offers me wise thoughts toward the healthy resolution of my challenges. It is the part of me that observes my life without judgment or desire and leads me to a peaceful existence that can be found only in acceptance of what is at any moment.

When my ego and this sacred voice are aligned, I feel content, even though my life is not how I thought it would be or as I ever wanted it to be. When the wisdom of our sacred voice is guiding us, and when our ego is motivated by faith rather than by fear, life is better.

OUR SOUL

At the moment of our death, our bodies consistently demonstrate a twenty-one-gram weight loss. Although there is no scientific evidence to substantiate or disprove this, it is believed that the twenty-one grams (about the size of a dime) are our eternal souls leaving our bodies. The existence, or not, of an eternal soul is part of a greater question: Is there a God? The answer to this question is a personal one that tremendously influences how we interact in the world and with whom.

Humans are curious by nature, with an innate desire to make sense of our world. It is the nonmaterial aspect that eludes us most. Albert Einstein said, "If God created the world, his primary concern was certainly not to make its understanding easy for us." Like most aspects of life that have multiple and contrasting points of view, the doubt about the existence of God is used to manipulate. Organized religion offers the means to minimize doubt with the support of a congregation and the collective worship of their common belief in God.

Spirituality is personal. It is our spiritual nature and private relationship with what we believe to be true about God. Atheism is a spiritual belief. Ultimately each of us gets to choose what we believe, and no matter what we call it, it forms our spiritual understanding of the aspect of life that can never be definitively proven. It is our most important belief that influences everything we do. Jesuit priest Pierre Teilhard de Chardin offers, "You are not a human being having a spiritual experience. You are a spiritual being having a human experience."

What I have learned in my personal quest for answers as I sought to best understand our fractured world is that our humanness makes us the same. It is the health of our spirituality that makes us different. I know that my spiritual growth has nothing to do with anyone else. Franciscan Friar Richard Rohr teaches us that "authentic spirituality is always about changing you. It's not about trying to change anyone else." I believe that our immortal soul is more important than anything about our material world.

Material wealth can offer comfort with more and better options, but the outcome and the quality of life as we live through a troubling challenge have nothing to do with wealth. No matter one's life circumstances or how another's life may appear better or easier, no one is immune to trauma, feelings of disappointment, loss, fear, self-doubt, sadness, inadequacy, or feeling overwhelmed. Our best life is lived with peace and contentment, which has nothing to do with the amount of worldly possessions we have and everything to do with the strength of our spirituality.

The more spiritually focused we become, the more the criteria for our choices change. The desire for material wealth becomes secondary to our spiritual growth. The pleasure of material wealth without a spiritual component is a fleeting sense of happiness and creates a constant state of needing more to sustain it. An attribute of spiritual strength is a state of gratitude for life itself and for our relationships. Material gifts are an added pleasure but are not a requirement for our happiness.

Much like our physical body, our soul needs to be fed. Food for the soul is our chosen activities that prove to enrich our spiritual beliefs and enhance our self-awareness. The strength of our spirituality and self-awareness provides us with just what we need to survive life's inherent challenges.

AFTERTHOUGHTS

I believe that the most important message in this book is that unless we develop a conscious connection with ourselves, we can
never know the relative ease that can exist when we walk into a
room of strangers or the relative confidence with which we can
make hard decisions. There is always an uncomfortable feeling
when encountering an unknown, but living the uncomfortable
with an inner connection means we are never alone in anything
we decide or do. I liken it to walking through life with unwavering
faith that no matter what happens, I'll be OK.

Time is our most precious resource. It is like our breath: without it we die. The thing about time is that it passes somewhat unnoticed until we look in the mirror and suddenly see its effects; it
is then that we know how valuable it is. There is a common belief
that time heals all wounds, that we waste time and time flies. At my
age, I have accrued enough time to confirm that time does fly, and
as it passes, we learn to appreciate it better because we understand
that we can never know how much we have left to live. I believe that
love, not time, is the healer of life and that time is never wasted
because each moment of time is filled with something that feeds
our consciousness and memory. Knowing this, I am reminded that
everything about life comes back to our free will to choose what

we will do with the time we are given. Spending time with others and investing in our relationships define our life. Time is the most generous gift we can offer to another. It can't be bought or made. It is a finite part of our existence that we choose to share with another. Knowing, forming a connection with, and valuing ourselves can only ensure that we will spend our time wisely with those who prove to enrich our lives.

I will leave you with something more to think about. In our world today, we have created convenient time-saving products using virtual reality. We can now exercise at home with a trainer, attend a therapy appointment, see a doctor, go to college, and play multiuser games without being in the presence of another person. Brick-and-mortar stores are being replaced by websites, and business offices are becoming fewer, with employees working remotely from their homes. Voice communication is being replaced with text and email. It is important that we use technology but that we do not become technology. We are becoming more isolated, with fewer in-person conversations and physical contact. I do not dispute the time-saving benefit and efficiency of our technological world, but virtual relationships can never replace the benefits of real interactions. Recent studies have concluded that hugs reduce the harmful effects of depression, stress, and high blood pressure. Real interactions are a necessity for our well-being. We can never allow technology to make us so dependent that we stop thinking for ourselves or lose our real-life connection with ourselves and each other.

If you are reading this, thank you. I hope it offered you thought-provoking insights that encourage your own personal pursuit of a good life.

ONE LAST THING

When I read the following verse, I had to include it here because it beautifully summarizes the benefits of valuing and loving yourself. As I researched its origin to properly credit the author, I learned that some believe it was penned by Charlie Chaplin on his seventieth birthday and that others believe it is an English translation of a Portuguese translation of an English book written by Kim and Alison McMillen titled *When I Loved Myself Enough*. The text has since been changed again into the version that's primarily found online and that follows here.

Note to the author: well done!

As I began to love myself I found that anguish and emotional suffering are only warning signs that I was living against my own truth. Today, I know, this is "AUTHENTICITY".

As I began to love myself I understood how much it can offend somebody. As I try to force my desires on this person, even though I knew the time was not right and the person was not ready for it, and even though this person was me. Today I call it "RESPECT".

As I began to love myself I stopped craving for a different life, and I could see that everything that surrounded me was inviting me to grow. Today I call it "MATURITY".

As I began to love myself I understood that at any circumstance, I am in the right place at the right time, and everything happens at the exactly right moment. So I could be calm. Today I call it "SELF-CONFIDENCE".

As I began to love myself I quit stealing my own time, and I stopped designing huge projects for the future. Today, I only do what brings me joy and happiness, things I love to do and that make my heart cheer, and I do them in my own way and in my own rhythm. Today I call it "SIMPLICITY".

As I began to love myself I freed myself of anything that is no good for my health—food, people, things, situations, and everything that drew me down and away from myself. At first I called this attitude a healthy egoism. Today I know it is "LOVE OF ONESELF".

As I began to love myself I quit trying to always be right, and ever since I was wrong less of the time. Today I discovered that is "MODESTY".

As I began to love myself I refused to go on living in the past and worry about the future. Now, I only live for the moment, where EVERYTHING is happening. Today I live each day, day by day, and I call it "FULFILLMENT".

As I began to love myself I recognized that my mind can disturb me and it can make me sick. But As I connected it to my heart, my mind became a valuable ally. Today I call this connection "WISDOM OF THE HEART".

We no longer need to fear arguments, confrontations or any kind of problems with ourselves or others. Even stars collide, and out of their crashing new worlds are born. Today I know that is "LIFE"!

FROM THE AUTHOR

I have lived enough years to want to be younger and to know what I know now for a do-over. But a do-over of my life won't result in me being the person I am, nor will I enjoy the pleasure of the people in my life today who I love. Besides, who would I be if I hadn't live the life I have lived? Somehow, through it all, I now not only love myself but also like who I am today. I can more easily accept each day as it is, with a promise to myself to do better as I learn more. I also know that nothing and no one is perfect, and normal for anything no longer exists; it never did.

I have read self-help books and spiritual literature, gone to workshops promising the answers to living a good life, attended church services, earned certifications in coaching and energy-based therapies, learned from my Christian friends, paid psychics, and studied astrology. I realized that just living my life is what teaches me what I need to know to live my best life. As long as I have faith and know that no matter what happens, I will never abandon myself, I will be OK. Nothing about my life matters more than my commitment to my own well-being. Everything starts from there.

My first book, *You Can't Know What You Don't Know Until You Know It*, tells too much about my life challenges but supports my belief that just living our lives teaches us what we need to know to survive the perils we encounter. It is strange how pain teaches us, and if we can live through the pain until it subsides, the aha moments are euphoric.

I wish you many aha moments. May you have clarity, confidence, and courage in all you choose to do and don't do.

ABOUT THE AUTHOR

Donna Levesque is a certified life coach passionate about helping people create the lives they desire by learning to love and accept themselves. For the past thirty years, she has worked as a corporate researcher and analyst. She is the author *of Realizations "Developing Self-Awareness"* and the memoir *You Can't Know What You Don't Know Until You Know It*. Levesque holds certificates in several healing modalities and regularly practices yoga and meditation. She lives on an island in New England with her family and dog, Bentley, and can be found at some point each day walking along the shore with one of her friends, sharing thoughts and finding peace in nature.

Made in the USA
Middletown, DE
21 February 2020